Christina
Aguilera

Morgan Talmadge

HIGH
interest
books

Scholastic Inc.
New York / Toronto / London / Auckland / Sydney
Mexico City / New Delhi / Hong Kong
Danbury, Connecticut

Book Design: Nelson Sa
Contributing Editor: Jennifer Ceaser

Photo Credits: Cover © Fitzroy Barrett/Globe Photos Inc.; p. 4 © Everett Collection; p. 7 © Henry McGee/Globe Photos Inc.; p. 8 © Jeff Spicer/Globe Photos Inc.; pp. 11, 13 © Everett Collection; p. 14 © Jeff Spicer/Globe Photos Inc.; pp. 17, 19 © Milan Ryba/Globe Photos Inc.; p. 20 © Andrea Renault/Globe Photos Inc.; p. 25 © Fitzroy Barrett/Globe Photos Inc.; p. 26 © Robert Hepler/Everett Collection; p. 29 © Alec Michael/Globe Photos Inc.; p. 31 © Corbis; p. 33 © Andrea Renault/Globe Photos Inc.; p. 34 © Fitzroy Barrett/Globe Photos Inc.; p. 37 © Robert Hepler/Everett Collection; p. 39 © Fitzroy Barrett/Globe Photos Inc.

Library of Congress Cataloging-in-Publication Data

Talmadge, Morgan.
  Christina Aguilera / by Morgan Talmadge.
    p. cm.—(Celebrity bios)
  Includes bibliographical references and index.
  ISBN 0-516-23422-6 (lib. bdg.)—ISBN 0-516-23584-2 (pbk.)
  1. Aguilera, Christina, 1980—Juvenile literature. 2. Singers—United States—Biography—Juvenile literature. [1. Aguilera, Christina, 1980- 2. Singers. 3. Women—Biography.] I. Title. II. Series.

ML3930.A36 T35 2000
782.42164 '092—dc21
[B]

                                                    00-034570

CONTENTS

1 Who's That Girl?   5

2 Ambitious Aguilera   15

3 A Star's Life   27

Timeline   40

Fact Sheet   43

New Words   44

For Further Reading   46

Resources   47

Index   48

About the Author   48

CHAPTER ONE

WHO'S THAT GIRL?

"Singing has always been a huge part of me. It's always been a love and a release."
—Christina in *Fanzine*

At the 42nd Annual Grammy Awards, competition in the category of Best New Artist was especially fierce. The nominees for that award included Macy Gray, Christina Aguilera, and Britney Spears. Many people felt sure that Britney would win the award. After all, her album . . . *Baby, One More Time* had sold more than eleven million copies! But when the winner was announced, it was not Britney Spears.

Christina Aguilera won for Best New Artist at the 42nd Annual Grammy Awards.

The winner of the Grammy Award for Best New Artist of 2000 was Christina Aguilera!

Ten years earlier, Christina had watched Mariah Carey win a Grammy Award for Best New Artist of 1990. "Best New Artist was the category that I would always single out as being . . . my dream nomination," Christina told MTV. "It's kind of a dream come true."

Many of Christina's dreams have come true. Her combination of hard work, dedication, and talent have made her one of today's most exciting pop music stars!

THE EARLY YEARS

Christina Maria Aguilera was born in Staten Island, New York, on December 18, 1980. Her parents are Fausto Aguilera, a sergeant in the U.S. Army, and Shelly Kearns, a homemaker and a violinist/pianist. Christina's father is Ecuadorian American and her mother is Irish American. As Christina grew up, Fausto's

Christina Aguilera is close to her mother (left), her sister Rachel (center), and stepsister Stephanie (right).

career required him to work at several different Army bases. He took his family with him each time he moved. As a toddler, Christina lived all over the world—in Japan, France, Texas, and New Jersey.

Christina's parents divorced when she was six years old. Christina moved with her mother and her baby sister, Rachel, to Wexford, Pennsylvania. Wexford, a suburb of Pittsburgh, was where Christina's grandmother lived. In Wexford, Christina's mother met and married James Kearns, a paramedic.

YOUNG PERFORMER

Christina began singing when she was just a toddler. One of her favorite albums was the soundtrack to the movie *The Sound of Music*. Christina memorized every song on the album. She laid a towel on the floor and pretended that it was the stage. She used a baton as her "ikaphone"—her childhood word for microphone. Even at a very young age, Christina had a large vocal range (the ability to sing very low or very high notes).

Christina's mother, Shelly, entered six-year-old Christina in local talent shows around Pittsburgh. Friends and neighbors also could count on little Christina to perform at neighborhood block parties. "I've never seen anybody so focused," Christina's mom recalled in *Rolling Stone*. "If there wasn't a block party or somewhere for her to sing, she'd get irritable."

Christina's fans love her unique style.

RUNNER-UP

At age eight, Christina landed a spot on the television talent show "Star Search." Christina performed "The Greatest Love of All" for the competition. The song had been a huge hit for Whitney Houston, one of Christina's favorite singers. Unfortunately, Christina lost to an older boy in her performance category. Christina was very upset. "Tears were running down my face . . . [it was] awful," she told *Rolling Stone*.

Losing on "Star Search" did not stop Christina's desire to be a performer. She bought a sound system with the money she won as a runner-up. She used that system to perform in parks and in other outdoor locations. At age ten, Christina sang the national anthem at sporting events for Pittsburgh teams, including the Steelers and the Penguins.

A DATE WITH MICKEY

In 1990, Christina auditioned for the Disney TV series, "Mickey Mouse Club." She tried out at an open audition in Pittsburgh, but she was not chosen. Still, she made an impression on the producers of the

The cast of "Mickey Mouse Club" get together. Christina is the one in the circle.

show. Two years later, twelve-year-old Christina was asked to audition again for the TV show. This time, she got the part!

Christina joined a show that had an incredible cast. Other performers on "Mickey Mouse Club" included J. C. Chasez and Justin Timberlake of 'N Sync, Britney Spears, and Keri Russell. "[Britney and I] totally looked up to Keri Russell," Christina remembered in an interview with *Teen People*. "She was sixteen, Britney was eleven, and I was twelve. We were always touching [Keri's] hair. We were such little dorks!"

Christina was part of the cast of "Mickey Mouse Club" for the next two years. Working on the show was not easy. Christina had to travel back and forth between her home in Pennsylvania and Orlando, Florida, where the show was taped. Filming "Mickey Mouse Club" meant hours of practice—not only for singing, but for dancing and acting, as well. Still,

Christina loved doing it. "It was a great way to grow up," she recalled in *Vibe*. "I loved being around kids who had the same passions I did."

THE PRICE OF FAME

Young Christina's career was taking off. She was known in Wexford as "the little girl with the big voice." But not everyone appreciated

Christina's growing fame. "My elementary school days were terrible. The other kids couldn't accept me as a singer," Christina recalled in *Seventeen*. She ended up switching elementary schools because it was so difficult for her to fit in with her classmates.

As she became better known on "Mickey Mouse Club," Christina started having problems with the kids at Marshall Middle School, too. "Kids didn't know how to deal with seeing [me] on TV," she told Rolling Stone. Things got so bad that classmates were threatening to beat up Christina and to slash her mother's tires.

In spite of the threats, Christina refused to give up her career. "My dream of becoming a recording artist kept me going," she told *Teen People*. After she finished the eighth grade, Christina's family decided to have her schooled at home. With the help of a tutor, she earned a high-school diploma.

Christina was part of the cast of
"Mickey Mouse Club" for two years.

CHAPTER TWO

AMBITIOUS AGUILERA

"It makes me feel good that I trusted my instincts. I've always had a vision of where I want to go."

—Christina in *Teen People*

In 1994, "Mickey Mouse Club" was canceled, but Christina kept right on singing. In 1997, she performed at international singing competitions all over Asia and Europe. Her manager, Steve Kurtz, traveled with her. In early 1998, Kurtz helped Christina record a demo tape to send to record companies. They sent the tape to Ron Fair, an executive at RCA Records. Fair

Christina has performed at international singing competitions all over Europe and Asia.

was blown away. "She is a genius of singing," Fair told *Rolling Stone*. "She was put on this Earth to sing." Fair was so impressed that RCA offered Christina a recording contract.

At about the same time, Christina's manager heard that Disney was looking for someone to record a song for the animated movie *Mulan*. Christina quickly recorded the Whitney Houston song "I Wanna Run To You" in her living room and rushed the tape to Disney. Disney executives were amazed by Christina's voice. They immediately chose Christina to sing the theme to *Mulan*—a song called "Reflections."

A NOTE THAT CHANGED EVERYTHING

Christina's RCA contract was put on hold while she made arrangements to record "Reflections." It was a perfect song to show off Christina's amazing vocal range. In the song, Christina hits the note E above high C. The

Christina signs her self-titled album for fans.

high E is considered a very difficult note for the human voice. "[It was] the note that changed my life," Christina told *Wall of Sound*.

When *Mulan* was released in June 1998, "Reflections" became an instant hit—climbing to number fifteen on the music charts. Later that year, the song was nominated for a Golden Globe Award for Best Original Song.

Did you know?

When Christina went to the prom at her boyfriend's high school, the disc jockey played "Genie in a Bottle."

SETTING THE STAGE

Thanks to the success of "Reflections," Christina was able to work with some of the music industry's best songwriters and producers on her debut album. These talented people had created hit songs for many pop stars, including 'N Sync, Brandy, and Monica.

RCA wasted no time in setting the stage for Christina's new album. Before releasing the record, the label set up a series of special concerts for Christina. In these small concerts, she sang in front of radio executives and people in the music industry. These performances showed that Christina's voice was the real thing and wasn't created in a sound studio.

Christina also appeared on national television, performing on "The Tonight Show" and

Christina Aguilera went double platinum in its first week of release.

Ambitious Aguilera

"Late Night with David Letterman." Internet sites were created where fans could hear Christina's music and talk about her in chat rooms. Audiences were amazed by Christina's powerful voice. People wanted to know if she had a CD, and where they could buy it. It was time for RCA to release Christina's first single.

LOOK WHO'S NUMBER ONE!
In June 1999, the single "Genie in a Bottle" was released. All the hard work that RCA had done

to promote Christina paid off. Within one month, "Genie in a Bottle" was the number-one song in the country. In two months, the single went platinum, selling 1 million copies.

The video for "Genie in a Bottle" shows a summer scene. It features Christina on a beach in a cutoff top and shorts. It displays Christina's great dance moves. The video looks like summer, but it actually was filmed on a cold spring night on a beach in Malibu, California. The entire crew wore heavy coats and scarves, but Christina and her dancers had to pretend to be hanging in the summer heat.

The video for "Genie in a Bottle" was an instant hit on MTV's "Total Request Live" (TRL), the daily series hosted by Carson Daly. "I'm honestly impressed [with Christina], she has a really remarkable voice," Daly said. "Genie in a Bottle" became MTV's fourth-most-requested video and stayed in the "Total Request Live" top ten for most of the summer.

When Christina performs live, it's easy to see that her amazing voice is the real thing.

RIGHT TO THE TOP

On August 24, 1999, Christina's album, *Christina Aguilera*, was released. Thanks to the enormous success of "Genie in a Bottle," the album zoomed to the top of the charts. The album sold more than 250,000 copies in its first week of release. Just one month after *Christina Aguilera* was released, it was certified double platinum (an album that sells 2 million copies).

Sales were not the only high point of Christina's huge success. Music critics also were impressed. *Time* magazine called her "one of the most strikingly gifted singers to come along since Mariah Carey."

Christina soon began appearing on magazine covers, such as *Teen People,* and on TV shows, including "The Tonight Show." Ice-skater Tara Lipinski even chose to skate to "Genie in a Bottle" for one of her routines.

CHRISTINA EVERYWHERE

Christina's enormous success opened many doors for her. Following the release of her album, Christina joined TLC's tour as their opening act. She performed for the president and the first lady at the White House on a "Christmas at the White House" TV special. The president also asked her to sing at the White House on New Year's Eve, but Christina had to decline. She already was scheduled to perform for MTV that night. Christina also appeared on "Saturday Night Live," at the Miss USA Pageant, and during halftime at Super Bowl XXXIV in January 2000.

REACHING NEW HEIGHTS

Christina had a great beginning to the new millennium. Her second single, "What a Girl Wants," became the first number-one single of 2000. Like "Genie in a Bottle," "What a

CHRISTINA AGUILERA

Girl Wants" was a huge hit on the radio and on MTV. With the success of the new single, *Christina Aguilera* went platinum seven times over.

Then, in February 2000, Christina's success became even sweeter. She was nominated for two Grammy Awards—Best New Artist and Best Female Pop Vocal Performance. Christina beat out Britney Spears to win the Best New Artist Grammy. "I was overwhelmed, shocked, and overjoyed all at the same time," the nineteen-year-old Christina told *Teen People*. "That was the award I wanted since I was a little girl. When I was eight or nine, my mom even made me a fake Grammy."

With a real Grammy in hand, Christina went on to pick up even more awards. She won the World Music Award for Best New Female Artist. She took home the Favorite Female New Artist and the Favorite Single (for "Genie in a Bottle") trophies from the Blockbuster Awards.

Christina wore a stunning dress at the Grammy Awards.

Teen People honored Christina as Best New Artist. She was named New Entertainer of the Year at the 2000 American Latino Media Arts Awards. And Christina had the honor of being the only woman asked to perform on the VH1 all-male singing special "Men Strike Back," which aired in April 2000.

CHAPTER THREE

A STAR'S LIFE

"All I want to do is be normal. But really, it's other people who won't let me be that way."
—**Christina in *YM***

Christina may be a huge star, but she's the first one to admit that being famous can be difficult. Many times Christina finds herself defending what she sings, says, does, or wears in public. "Being nineteen does put more pressure on you if you want to be taken seriously as an artist," Christina told *YM*. "You have to be way sharper than anybody else, because people expect you to be this bubblegum airhead."

Still, Christina can't protect herself against everybody. One nasty incident took place when Christina presented an award to rapper Marshall Mathers, known as Eminem, at the

Christina sports curly locks at the Billboard Awards.

MTV European Video Music Awards. Eminem told the crowd that he wanted to take Christina home rather than the award. Christina claimed she didn't hear what he said. "I didn't even know about it until I got offstage," she explained to MTV. Several months later, Eminem released a song with rude lyrics about Christina. "It's disgusting, and offensive and, above all, it's not true," Christina said.

Christina's feelings were deeply hurt by Eminem's rude song. "It's really difficult sometimes not to take it personally, because those people don't know you," she told MTV. Unfortunately, it is not the only time Christina has had to deal with ugly things being said about her. One of the hardest parts of her busy life is trying to ignore gossip and rumors.

RUMORS

Once Christina visited the "TRL" set when Carson Daly was on vacation. At the time, Daly

Christina smiles for the camera at the MTV European Video Music Awards.

was dating Jennifer Love Hewitt. Christina left a message for Daly telling him that she was sorry she didn't get to see him. The press found out about the note. *USA Today* ran an article about Christina's big crush on Daly. The rumor did not cause any lasting damage. Christina and Daly remain friends.

Other gossip suggested that Christina was fighting with Britney Spears. She wasn't. In fact, Christina told *Entertainment Weekly*, "If anything, we'll probably do a collaboration." Some rumors have linked her romantically with Nick Carter, Enrique Iglesias, or Lance Bass. There also have been instances where people pretended to be Christina in chat rooms on the Internet. On Christina's official Web site, there is an entire page devoted to The Rumor Mill. You can log on and find out which rumors are true and which ones are false! (For the record, she claims that she has not dated any of the boys mentioned above.)

Christina and Enrique Iglesias sang together at the halftime show for Super Bowl 2000.

TOO BUSY FOR LOVE

Some of Christina's fans might think she could have any guy she wants. However, Christina's nonstop schedule makes it hard for her to date. If she's not touring, she is almost always making a public appearance, recording new music, or filming a video. Such a busy schedule makes it hard to find time for anyone special in her life. "There are a few people around me . . . giving me love and support and affection," Christina told *Teen People*, "but right now, my career is my boyfriend."

Christina has mentioned a few guys on whom she's had crushes. "I'd rather date a rocker than a boy-band guy," she told *YM*. Christina told *Rolling Stone* that Fred Durst, the lead singer for Limp Bizkit, asked her to be his date for the MTV Video Music Awards. She went to the awards show, but not with Durst. Christina explained that her record company would not allow her to go with him. She also said she has had crushes

Christina looks fabulous at the MTV Video Music Awards.

on Mark McGrath of Sugar Ray and on British singer Robbie Williams.

Recently, Christina has been linked to dancer Jorge Santos. She told *Seventeen* of their relationship: "I'm head over heels in love, but it's really hard with all this travel and my crazy lifestyle."

WHAT A GIRL WEARS

There may not be any room for a boyfriend in Christina's life, but she always finds time to shop. Christina has a stylist, but the young singer always has a say in what she wears. For inspiration, Christina looks to other artists who are on the cutting edge, including Janet Jackson and Madonna. "I want to be a pop girl with an edge. I like a bit of toughness with my girlieness," she told *InStyle*. For the "Genie in a Bottle" video, Christina was costumed completely in Dolce & Gabbana, the very hip Italian designers. "The patterns are really cool. You can mix and match whatever," she told *Teen People*. She also likes shopping at smaller clothing stores, such as Bebe and Miu Miu.

Christina looked great in a metallic Versace dress when she accepted her Grammy Award for Best New Artist. That is not surprising—Versace designers spent twenty-eight hours fitting her for the slinky outfit!

Christina and Lisa Lopez of TLC pose together at the ASCAP 2000 Music Awards.

Christina never goes out in public without eyeliner and mascara. "There are always random photographers," she explained to *InStyle*, so it's important that she look her best. She also loves "glossy, really wet lips," and favors MAC lipgloss.

MOVING AHEAD

Christina's experience on "Mickey Mouse Club" gave her practice with being famous. As long as Christina can remember, people have been asking her for her autograph. "I was signing autographs when I barely knew how to spell my name," she told *Teen People*. As a teenager, Christina Aguilera has sold millions of albums and has won many awards. She has had three top-twenty singles. She has gotten to work with some of her greatest idols. She kicked off a solo tour in July 2000 with Destiny's Child as the opening act. So what more could this girl possibly want?

Christina looks lovely at the American Music Awards.

The year 2000 was a busy one for Christina. She recorded two separate albums in the studio. The first was a record of Christmas songs, which featured a sixty-piece

orchestra. It included the song "Climb Ev'ry Mountain" from *The Sound of Music*. It also featured a duet with one of Christina's idols, Etta James. On tour, Christina does the song "At Last," a song made famous by Etta James. Christina also recorded a TV special to go along with the record.

The second album Christina recorded is her first Spanish-language recording. The album is Christina's way of honoring her Ecuadorian heritage. "The Spanish side of me is something I'm really interested in tapping into and getting to explore," she told MTV. The Spanish album features some translations of her American hits, including "Genio Atrapado," the Spanish-language version of "Genie in A Bottle." The album also features new Spanish songs, as well.

With all her musical success, it's natural that Christina has considered going into acting. "I've been offered a few movie parts . . . but

Christina steps out at the American Latin Music Awards.

[right now] I have to really concentrate on singing," she explained in an AOL interview. Christina also is thinking about writing and producing music in the future. "I trust my own instincts," she told *Time*. "I want to do serious stuff, too, stuff that conveys maturity." There's plenty of time for young Christina to become the next Mariah Carey or Whitney Houston. With such an amazing voice, it's clear that Christina Aguilera is here to stay.

TIMELINE

1980
- Christina Maria Aguilera is born on December 18.

1986
- Christina's parents divorce. Christina moves to Wexford, Pennsylvania, with her mother and her younger sister, Rachel.

1989
- Christina appears on "Star Search"—and loses.

1990
- Christina auditions in Pittsburgh for Disney's "Mickey Mouse Club," but does not get cast.
- Christina sings the national anthem at local sporting events for Pittsburgh teams, including the Steelers and the Penguins.

1993
- Christina auditions again for Disney's "Mickey Mouse Club" and is cast.

1998
- Christina records a demo tape.
- Disney chooses Christina to sing "Reflections" for the soundtrack of the movie *Mulan*.

TIMELINE

1999
- Christina is signed to a recording contract by RCA Records.
- In June, "Genie in a Bottle," is released as a single from Christina's debut album. Within one month the song hits number one.
- Christina's self-titled album is released in August and hits number one.
- Christina appears at Lilith Fair in Ohio and Pennsylvania.
- In November, Christina joins TLC's tour as the opening act.
- In December, Christina performs an exclusive show for the student body of Franklin High School in Milwaukee, Wisconsin.

2000
- Christina appears in the halftime show for Super Bowl XXXIV.
- "What a Girl Wants" is released and zooms to number one on the charts.
- In February, Christina wins a Grammy Award for Best New Artist.
- Christina sings "Don't Make Me Love You" for the soundtrack to *The Next Best Thing,* starring Madonna.

TIMELINE

2000
- In May, Christina wins Favorite Female New Artist and Favorite Single (for "Genie In a Bottle") at the Blockbuster Awards.
- *Teen People* honors Christina as Best New Artist.
- Christina is named New Entertainer of the Year at the 2000 American Latino Media Arts Awards.
- Christina wins Best New Female Artist at the World Music Awards.
- In July, Christina kicks off her solo tour.

2001
- Christina records a remake of *Lady Marmalade* for the film *Moulin Rouge* with Lil' Kim, Mya, and Pink.
- Christina wins a Latin Grammy Award for Female Pop Vocal Album.

2002
- Christina releases her new album *Stripped*.

2003
- Christina tours with Justin Timberlake.

2004
- Christina wins Grammy Award for Best Female Pop Vocal Performance for *Beautiful*.

FACT SHEET

Name	Christina Maria Aguilera
Birthdate	December 18, 1980
Family	Father: Fausto Aguilera; Mother: Shelly Kearns; Stepfather: James Kearns, Younger Sister: Rachel ("Ro"); Half brother: Michael; Stepsister: Stephanie; Stepbrother: Casey
Birthplace	Staten Island, New York
Hair/Eyes	Blonde/Blue
Height	5' 2"
Sign	Sagittarius

Favorites

Foods	Fast food from McDonald's and Wendy's, Starbuck's Caff ˈocha, tacos
Musicians	Whitney Hou Mariah Carey, Etta James
Group	Limp Bizkit
Designers	Dolce & G bana, Versace
Hobbies	Spending time with her family, going on long drives with friends, watching movies
Items	Her *Hello Kitty!* collection

NEW WORDS

audition a try-out performance

chart a listing that ranks music sales

debut a performer's first appearance

demo tape a recording intended to show off a song or a performer to a record producer

double platinum record an award for an album that sells two million copies or more

duet a song for two performers

Grammy an award given in recognition of musical achievement

manager a person who supervises a musician's career

platinum record an award for an album that sells one million copies

pop relating to popular music

producer a person who supervises the production of a recording

record label a company that produces and sells records

single a song that is released separately from an album

soundtrack the music recorded for a movie

tour a series of concerts or appearances

vocal range how low or high you can sing

FOR FURTHER READING

Golden, Anna Louise. *Christina Aguilera.* New York: St. Martin's Press, Inc., 2000.

MacDermot, Molly. *Christina Aguilera: The Unofficial Book.* New York: Watson-Guptil, 2000.

Murphy, Catherine. *Christina Aguilera.* Kansas City, MO: Andrews & McMeel, 2000.

Robb, Jackie. *Christina Aguilera: An Unauthorized Biography.* New York: HarperCollins, 1999.

Christina Aguilera Official Web Site
www.christina-a.com
This official site includes a bio, fan club information, photos, tour information, and the latest news about Christina.

MTV Online
www.mtv.com
This is MTV's official Web site where you can check out photos, interviews, and the latest news and video clips featuring Christina.

Rock on the Net
www.rockonthenet.com/artists-a/
christinaaguilera.htm
This site includes a timeline, bio, and links to other Christina sites on the Web.

You can write to Christina at the following address:
The Official Christina Aguilera Fan Club
244 Madison Avenue, #314
New York, NY 10016

INDEX

A

Aguilera, Fausto, 6
American Latino Media
    Arts Awards, 25

B

Blockbuster Awards, 24

C

Christina Aguilera, 22, 24
"Christmas at the
    White House," 23

D

Daly, Carson, 21, 28, 30

E

Eminem, 27, 28

G

"Genie in a Bottle,"
    20, 21, 23, 35, 38
Golden Globe Award, 17
Grammy Award(s), 5, 6, 24, 35

K

Kearns, Shelly, 6, 8
Kurtz, Steve, 15

M

"Men Strike Back," 25
"Mickey Mouse Club,"
    10, 11, 13, 15, 36
MTV Europoean Video
    Music Awards, 28
Mulan, 16, 17

R

RCA Records, 15, 16,
    18–20
Russell, Keri, 11

S

"Saturday Night Live," 23
Spears, Britney, 5, 24, 30
"Star Search," 9, 10

T

Timberlake, Justin, 11

W

"What a Girl Wants," 23
World Music Award, 24

ABOUT THE AUTHOR

Morgan Talmadge is a freelance writer and soccer coach living in Mt. Vernon, Iowa.